GW01319774

To the reader:

Welcome to the DK ELT Grade [...]
different. They explore aspects [...]
history, geography, science … and a lot of other things. They
show the different ways people live now, and lived in the past.

These DK ELT Graded Readers give you material for
reading for information, and reading for pleasure. You are
using your English to do something real. The illustrations
will help you understand the text, and help bring the Reader
to life. Listen to the cassette or CD as well, and you can
really enter the world of the Olympic Games, the *Titanic*, or
the Trojan War … and a lot more. Choose the topics that
interest you, improve your English, and learn something …
all at the same time. Enjoy the series!

To the teacher:

This series provides varied reading practice at five levels of
language difficulty, from elementary to FCE level:
BEGINNER
ELEMENTARY A
ELEMENTARY B
INTERMEDIATE
UPPER INTERMEDIATE
The language syllabus has been designed to suit the factual
nature of the series, and includes a wider vocabulary range
than is usual with ELT readers: language linked with the
specific theme of each book is included and glossed.
The language scheme, and ideas for exploiting the material
(including the recorded material) both in and out of class are
contained in the Teacher's Resource Book. We hope you and
your students enjoy using this series.

A DORLING KINDERSLEY BOOK

 www.dk.com

Originally published as Eyewitness Reader
Bugs! Bugs! Bugs! in 1998 and adapted as an
ELT Graded Reader for Dorling Kindersley by

studio cactus ©

13 SOUTHGATE STREET   WINCHESTER   HAMPSHIRE   SO23 9DZ

Published in Great Britain by
Dorling Kindersley Limited
9 Henrietta Street, London WC2E 8PS

2 4 6 8 10 9 7 5 3 1

A CIP catalogue record for this book is
available from the British Library.

ISBN 0-7513-3162-7

Colour reproduction by Colourscan, Singapore
Printed and bound in China by L. Rex Printing Co., Ltd
Text film output by Ocean Colour, UK

The publisher would like to thank the following for
their kind permission to reproduce their photographs:
Key: t=top, b=below, l=left, r=right, c=centre

Biofotos: C. Andrew Henley 14–15; **Bruce Coleman:** Gerald
Cubitt 24br; M.P.L. Fogden 9bl; Peter Zabransky 17tr; **FLPA:** Larry
West 23br; **NHPA:** Stephen Dalton 12–13, 27tr; **OSF:** G.I. Bernard
29br; J.A.L. Cooke 15tr; **Planet Earth Pictures:** Brian Kenney
26–27; **Warren Photographic:** Kim Taylor 13cr.

Additional photography by Jane Burton, Neil Fletcher,
Frank Greenaway, Colin Keates, Harry Taylor,
Kim Taylor, Jerry Young

Jacket credit
Natural History Photographic Agency/Stephen Dalton

ELT Graded Readers

ELEMENTARY A

BUGS

Written by
Maureen
Haughton

Series Editor
Susan Holden

London • New York • Delhi • Sydney

Stag beetle

There are about one million different kinds of insects in the world. They live everywhere: in the Arctic, the Antarctic; in deserts; in and near water; underground, and in the mountains.

Dragonfly

They are not usually dangerous to humans, but some insects have stings that hurt. Others can cut your skin and make it bleed.

Some of the insect fossils in rocks are 300 million years old.

Some insects are vegetarians: they eat green plants and wood. But some of them eat other insects, even bigger ones. And some insects, like the praying mantis female, eat the male after mating!

Praying mantis

Weevil-hunting wasp

The praying mantis gets its name from the way it holds its front legs. These look like hands together in prayer.

It lives in warm climates all over the world: Southern Europe, Africa, South America, and Asia. Mantids (the plural of mantis) usually live alone. Other insects are afraid of them, because they catch them and eat them.

There are about 1,800 different kinds of mantids. Some are green or brown, and are very difficult to see on a leaf or a plant. Others look like colourful flowers – purple or blue.

The mantis does not hunt for food. It waits for other insects to come near, and does not move at all.

When another insect comes near, the mantis shoots out its front legs and holds the insect tight. The poor insect cannot escape because the mantis has little hooks on its legs. These help it to hold the insect. It starts eating the insect from the head, so the insect does not fight for long, but dies quickly. Some big mantids are strong enough to kill and eat frogs and birds.

The mantis also uses its long front legs to protect itself. Its legs are very sharp, and can cut the skin of a human being.

Some bugs hunt for food – not for themselves, but for their babies.

The wasp here is taking a weevil to its nest. Poor weevil!

A wasp's nest is made from a kind of paper. The wasp chews dead wood and the stems of plants, and mixes these with its saliva. The result, when dry, looks like grey paper.

Weevil-hunting wasp

This is what happens to the weevil. The wasp stings the weevil, but it doesn't kill it. It paralyzes it, so it cannot move. Then it pulls the weevil to its nest. This can be many metres away – a long way for a wasp!

The wasp then lays an egg in the nest, and goes away. When the larva comes out of the egg, it begins to eat the weevil. The weevil is excellent food.

The larva becomes very fat, and changes into a wasp. Then the cycle begins again.

Hairy food

The spider-hunting wasp catches very big spiders for its babies. The fight between a wasp and a bigger spider is exciting, but the result is always the same. The wasp is always the winner!

Ants are small, social insects. One ant has
very simple behaviour, but a lot of ants – a
colony – can behave very intelligently. They
are experts at collecting food. They grow
food, and they hunt for it, like humans.

Ants also live a long time.
A worker ant can live for seven
years, and a queen for fifteen
years. The workers look after
the queen.

Some ants produce acid that can kill another insect. When the insect is dead, the ants carry it back to their nest. If the insect is big, the ants sometimes cut it into two pieces, so that it is easier to move. This is happening in the picture here. The little ants are cutting up the big insect.

Not all ants eat meat: some are vegetarian, and eat leaves, and seeds, and fungus.

If you live in Europe, north Africa, the Middle East, or northwest India, you can often see dragonflies near water, especially near canals or ponds.

The life-cycle of a dragonfly is very long. The eggs develop in about three weeks, and a nymph comes out. This lives under the water for about two years. It moves under the water by jet propulsion. It catches small worms, but it can also eat bigger things, like tadpoles and little fish.

It grows most in summer, when the water is warm and there is a lot of food. The nymph turns into an adult dragonfly. This beautiful insect lives in the air for a few weeks, lays its eggs, and then dies.

Dragonflies eat most of the time! They are very good hunters, because they can see the "food" coming from all directions. This is because they have all-round vision from their big eyes.

Their legs hang down like little baskets, and they can hold onto the "food". They can catch small insects, and eat them, and fly ... all at the same time! But they take bigger insects to a resting place at the side of the pond to eat.

They can eat their own body weight in about half an hour! Think of this. Think of your own body weight! How many kilos is it? Then think of half those kilos ... Is it possible for you to eat that in half an hour?

Ancient insect
Dragonflies are very old – older than dinosaurs. They look the same now as 230 million years ago. The piece of rock here shows a perfect dragonfly shape, exactly the same as today's dragonflies.

An assassin is a professional killer – a murderer. In the Middle Ages, assassins used poisoned knives to kill people. The assassin bug uses poison too. Assassin bugs are expert killers!

There are about 2,500 different kinds of assassin bugs in the world. They can catch their food in different ways. Some of them run after their victim, and jump on it. Their feet are oily, and the victim cannot escape. Others wait quietly for the victim to come near, and then jump.

Kissing bugs
Some assassin bugs are called "kissing bugs" because they often bite people on their faces. This is probably because the skin on the face is soft, not because the bugs love people!

Assassin bugs produce a poison that they can inject into their victims. This poison does two things: it kills other insects and it turns the victims' insides into a kind of soup!

Then the assassin uses the pump in its head to suck the "soup" into its own digestive system. The poison does not hurt the assassin. It has a clever trick. It produces poison but it can also produce a non-poisonous fluid. This fluid cancels out the poison!

The assassin uses the non-poisonous liquid to wash its mouth after it injects poison into another insect.

It is easy to recognize the male stag beetle because of its jaws. However, stag beetles do not use these jaws to catch food. In fact, they are useless for catching and chewing. The beetles only use their jaws to fight with other male stag beetles during the mating season.

Look at the picture here. Two male stag beetles are fighting. They are probably fighting for a female beetle. They are using their jaws.

Short, sharp jaws

The male stag beetle has very long jaws, which look like the antlers of a stag. That is how it gets its name. The female stag beetle has smaller jaws, but they are stronger!

The stag beetle's jaws look very frightening, but in fact they are weak.

The fight is over when one beetle falls on its back. It gives up and stops fighting. The winner gets the female stag beetle!

*Monarch
butterfly
caterpillar*

Insects have dangerous lives! Other insects are often their enemies. And birds and animals often eat them, too. But they know how to protect themselves.

Many of them use special tricks. They use strong smells, bright colours, and bad tastes. Some of them even use poison.

Hoverfly

Click beetle

Other insects can jump in a special way, or they can imitate a different insect. They can do lots of things to stay alive.

Read about the insects on the next pages – see the different things they do to stay alive!

Postman butterfly caterpillar

Some people give shieldbugs a different name: stinkbugs. This is because they smell very bad; in fact, they stink! When an enemy is near, or they are in danger, they produce a very bad smell. Other insects and birds do not like this smell, and they keep away.

Shieldbugs stay near their babies, and look after them, so that more of them can live. This is very unusual, because generally insects are not good parents. Usually, a female insect lays her eggs, and flies away. But the shieldbug has a big, flat body like a shield. She uses this to protect her babies.

Here is a mother shieldbug and a lot of babies on a leaf. She is protecting them with her body. The babies, or nymphs, stay close together under the female's body. Other insects, and birds, cannot see them. When the nymphs move around a leaf, they all move together.

After a few weeks, the nymphs can look after themselves. They do not need their mother any more – and she dies.

Butterflies are very beautiful. You can find them almost all over the world. In Britain, there are about seventy different kinds, but in Malaysia, there are about a thousand. They like the hot, humid weather there!

Butterflies must protect themselves from their enemies. Many of them do this with bright colours. These monarch butterflies are orange. When they fly, they look like a fire or an explosion. This flash of colour frightens their enemies.

The monarch butterfly also tastes bad. This is because the monarch caterpillar eats a lot of milkweed. This is a plant that grows in open spaces and near roads. Milkweed contains poisons called cardenolides, and this poison gets into the caterpillar's body when it eats the milkweed.

These poisons do not kill the monarch caterpillar or butterfly, but they make other animals very sick. So the monarch's enemies learn not to eat it. They look for different food – and the monarch survives.

Changing faces

The butterfly lays eggs on a plant. When the caterpillars come out of the eggs a few days later, they eat the plant. After about a month, the caterpillar changes into a butterfly inside a hard "box" called a chrysalis.

*Tropical lappet
moth caterpillar*

Some caterpillars frighten their enemies with their bright colours. Others, like the one here, have different ways to protect themselves.

This caterpillar has long hairs all over its body. When an enemy tries to eat it, it gets a mouthful of hair! Very soon, other creatures learn not to eat this caterpillar!

The lappet moth caterpillar and the monarch both protect themselves. They do not fight their enemies: they frighten them.

Safety in numbers
Caterpillars often stay together in a group. When something frightens them, they all lift up their heads and move them at the same time! Their enemies cannot understand this, and usually go away.

This caterpillar grows very sharp spikes all over its body, even on its head. It also eats leaves that become poison inside its body. The poison does not hurt the caterpillar, but it makes birds very sick.

Some caterpillars try to look like something else. The swallowtail butterfly caterpillar looks like a bird dropping when it comes out of the egg. Later, it turns from black and white to bright green. Then, it has a horrible smell, like old pineapples, which birds and spiders do not like. A bad smell is very good protection against your enemies.

Postman butterfly caterpillar

Other insects protect themselves in different ways, too. Some of them use mimicry – this means that they look like something else, behave like something else, or make a noise like something else.

The thornbug is good at hiding, because it looks like a thorn on a branch. Imagine a rose bush with sharp thorns – and think how careful people are when they pick the roses in the garden!

Thorns can hurt!

A hungry bird will probably not notice the thornbug, or will think it is a thorn, so the insect is able to stay safe.

If there are a lot of thornbugs on one branch, they usually all look in the same direction, and they do not move at all. They look like a line of thorns.

That is why there are so many thornbugs around! They can protect themselves very well, and in a very simple way.

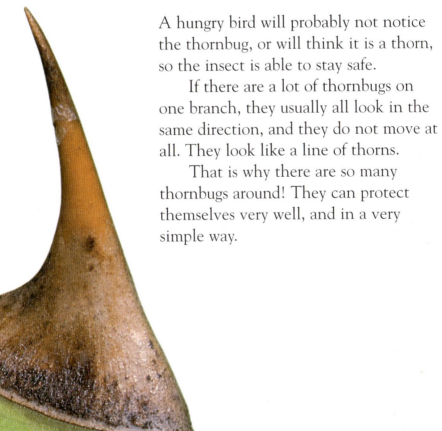

These click beetles jump to escape from their enemies. Perhaps you think that this is not especially clever – most insects can jump!

What is special about this? Well, read on! These click beetles have a special trick!

Most insects have a problem: if they land on their backs, they cannot turn over again. They lie on the ground and wave their legs in the air, so they are very easy to catch.

Click beetles, however, are special. If this happens, if they land on their backs, they can escape! They can contract the muscles in their heads and in the front part of their bodies. They can push themselves into the air again, and then they land on their feet.

If you touch a click beetle gently near its stomach, you can see these muscles contracting. It is trying to escape from you. It is trying to jump away and to land on its feet.

Be careful! Don't hurt it!

Flashing lights
Some click beetles in tropical countries can send out light signals. This light helps the beetle to find a mate. In some places, people use the beetles like torches.

Hoverflies use mimicry too. They look like hornets. Hornets are dangerous: they can sting, and some people have a lot of pain from a hornet sting. Because hornets are dangerous, birds do not often attack them.

Hoverflies do not sting, but their enemies often think that they are hornets, so they leave them alone. It is better to be safe than sorry!

The pictures on these two pages show two different insects.
They look almost the same, don't they?

Which is the hoverfly?

Which is the hornet?

Can you tell?

Look carefully!

Bug Facts

There are more than one million different kinds of insects in the world.

Some people call all insects "bugs". But in fact, only those insects that use sharp tubes, like drinking straws, to eat, are bugs.

All insects have six legs, but not all of them have wings all their lives.

Some insects use their legs to hear. Other insects use their feet to taste.

Some insects eat, and eat, and eat all the time when they are young. When they are adults, they don't eat anything at all.

Some insects have very good eyes. Their vision is excellent. They can see colours that people cannot see.